Moose
Happenings,

Moses

Written and Illustrated by
Gwenn Huot

To order additional copies of this book, contact:
Xlibris
844-714-8691
www.Xlibris.com
Orders@Xlibris.com

ISBN: Softcover   978-1-4363-6836-0
       Hardcover   978-1-4363-6837-7
       EBook   978-1-6641-4909-0

Library of Congress Control Number: 2008907962

Print information available on the last page

Rev. date: 12/18/2020

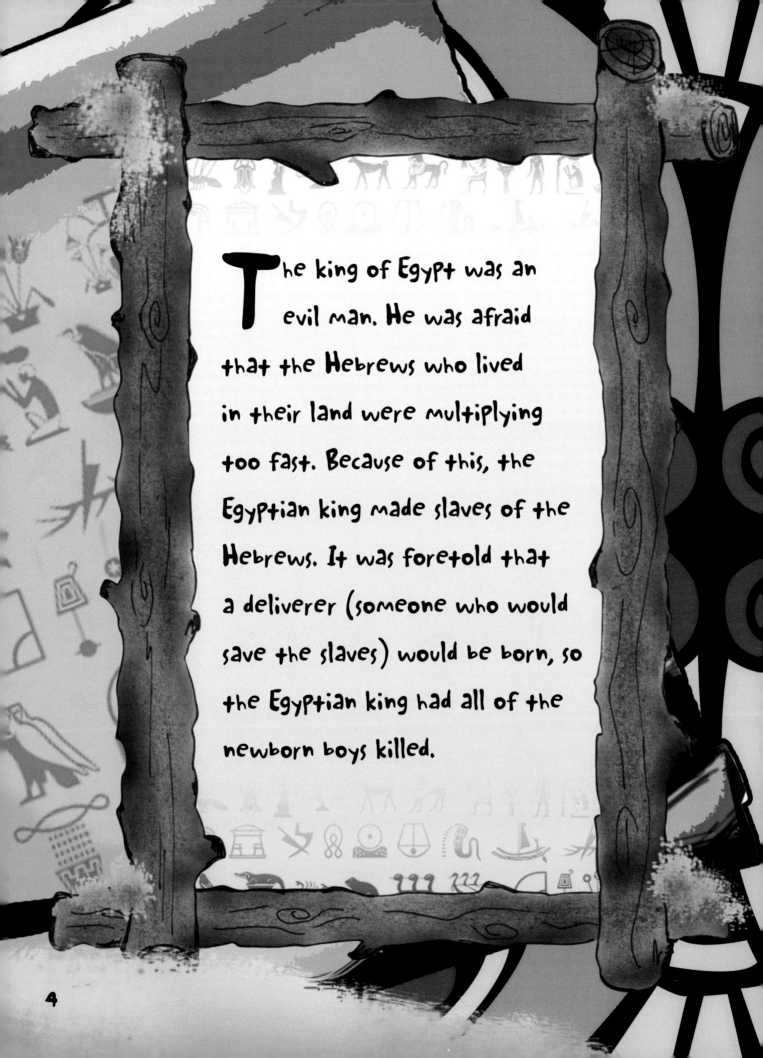

The king of Egypt was an evil man. He was afraid that the Hebrews who lived in their land were multiplying too fast. Because of this, the Egyptian king made slaves of the Hebrews. It was foretold that a deliverer (someone who would save the slaves) would be born, so the Egyptian king had all of the newborn boys killed.

The king's daughter, the
Princess, was wading in the
water one day.

The princess saw a basket with a baby in it, floating in the river. Someone had put their baby in the basket to try and save him from being killed. The princess fell in love with the baby and kept him.

She named him
Moses and raised
him like a prince.

Moses grew and saw how the Egyptian taskmasters were beating a man. Moses yelled at him to stop. When the taskmaster didn't stop, Moses killed him. Moses was cast out of Egypt and found a home across the desert.

One day Moses was out tending the sheep when he saw a bush that was on fire, but didn't burn. When Moses went to see it, God spoke to him. "Go back to Egypt and set your people free."

Moses returned to Egypt to tell the Pharaoh (the Egyptian king) to set his people free.

The Pharaoh wouldn't listen to Moses, so God sent one plague after another. Finally the Pharaoh set the Hebrews free.

Rivers turned to blood

Frogs

Swarms of gnats

Animals and people got sick

Locust

Hail

Darkness

Here Lies Moose-alamode

Death to first born

Moses led the people to the sea. God parted the sea and let the Hebrews walk right through the middle!

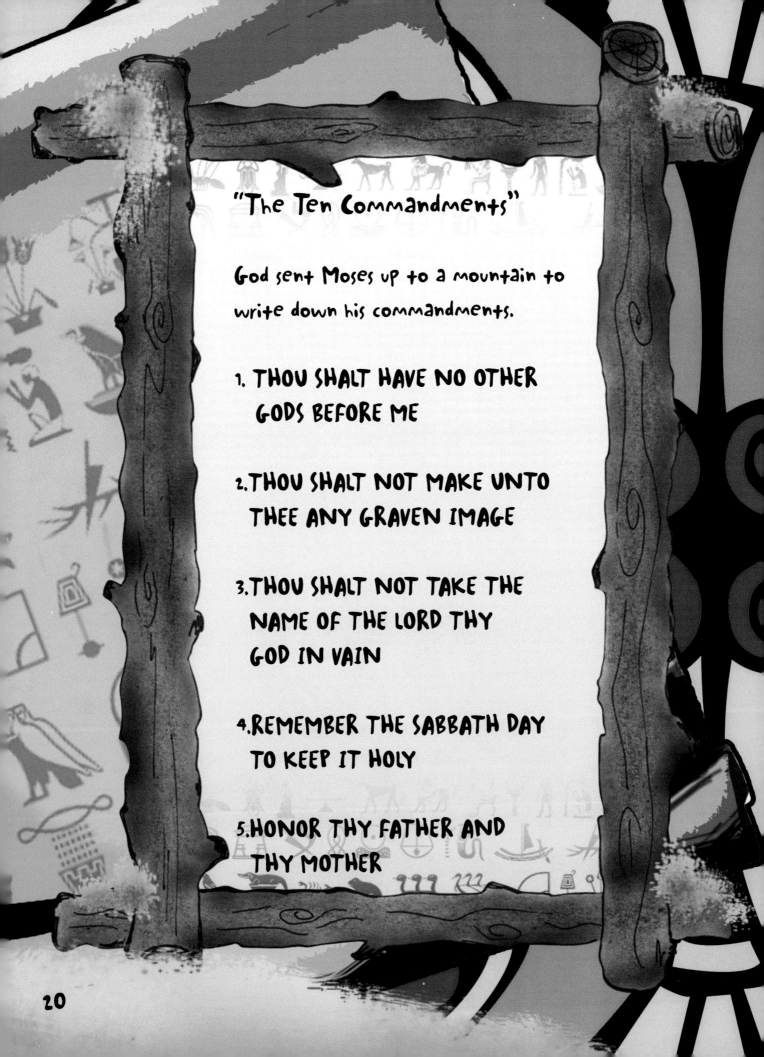

"The Ten Commandments"

God sent Moses up to a mountain to write down his commandments.

1. THOU SHALT HAVE NO OTHER GODS BEFORE ME

2. THOU SHALT NOT MAKE UNTO THEE ANY GRAVEN IMAGE

3. THOU SHALT NOT TAKE THE NAME OF THE LORD THY GOD IN VAIN

4. REMEMBER THE SABBATH DAY TO KEEP IT HOLY

5. HONOR THY FATHER AND THY MOTHER

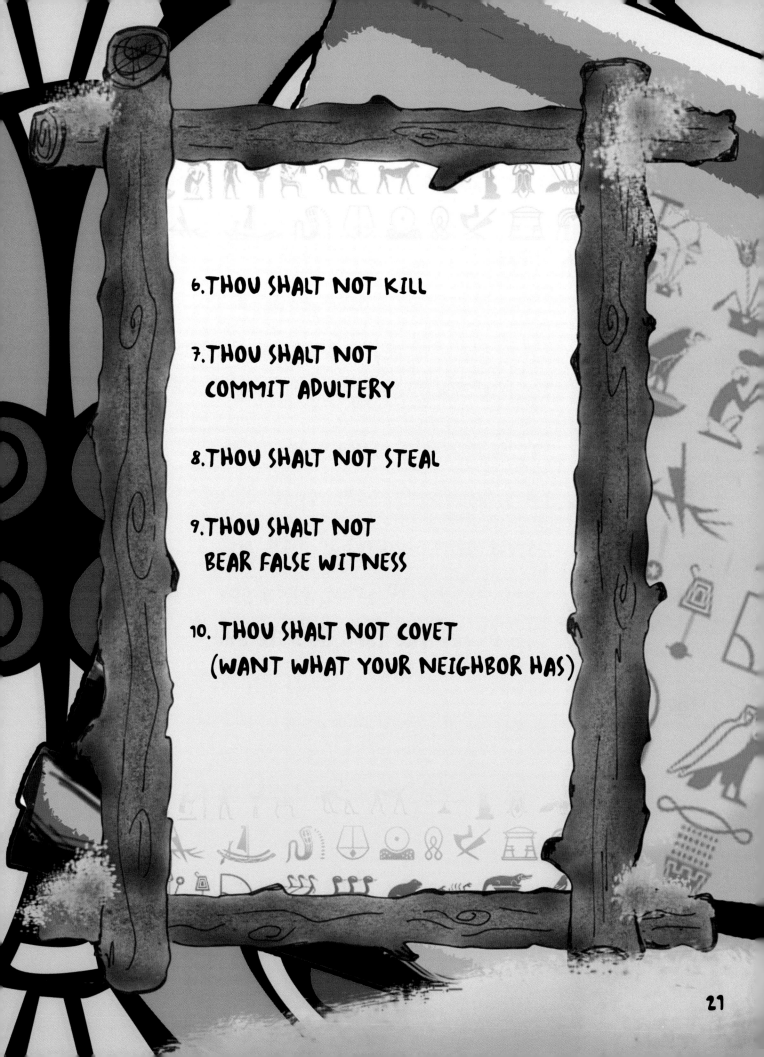

6. THOU SHALT NOT KILL

7. THOU SHALT NOT
   COMMIT ADULTERY

8. THOU SHALT NOT STEAL

9. THOU SHALT NOT
   BEAR FALSE WITNESS

10. THOU SHALT NOT COVET
    (WANT WHAT YOUR NEIGHBOR HAS)

The Hebrews disobeyed God many times after God did all of His miracles to save them, so God made them wander the dessert for 40 years until all of that generation had died. At the end of 40 years, they got to enter the land of milk and honey, where everything in the land was fruitful.

Acts 16:16-18

One day on our way to the place of prayer, we were met by a slave girl. She had a spirit in her that gave her the power to tell the future. The girl followed Paul and the rest of us and kept yelling. This went on for several days. Finally Paul got so upset that he turned and said to the spirit, "In the name of Jesus Christ, I order you to leave this girl alone!" At once the evil spirit left her.

"This is where the Bible stands on fortune-telling."

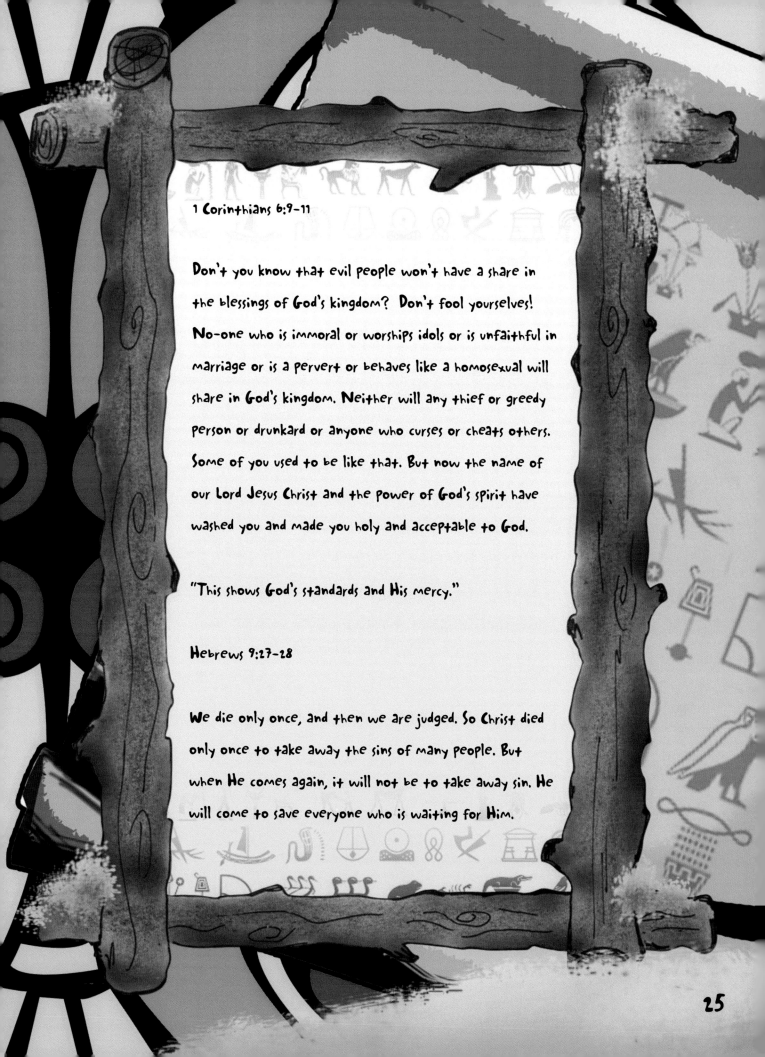

1 Corinthians 6:9-11

Don't you know that evil people won't have a share in the blessings of God's kingdom? Don't fool yourselves! No-one who is immoral or worships idols or is unfaithful in marriage or is a pervert or behaves like a homosexual will share in God's kingdom. Neither will any thief or greedy person or drunkard or anyone who curses or cheats others. Some of you used to be like that. But now the name of our Lord Jesus Christ and the power of God's spirit have washed you and made you holy and acceptable to God.

"This shows God's standards and His mercy."

Hebrews 9:27-28

We die only once, and then we are judged. So Christ died only once to take away the sins of many people. But when He comes again, it will not be to take away sin. He will come to save everyone who is waiting for Him.

James 5:16

If you have sinned, you should tell each other what you have done. Then you can pray for one another and be healed.

1 Peter 4:12-14

Dear friends, don't be surprised or shocked that you are going through testing that is like walking through fire. Be glad for the chance to suffer as Christ suffered. It will prepare you for even greater happiness when He makes his glorious return. Count it a blessing when you suffer for being a Christian.

This shows that God's glorious spirit is with you.